D1595759

A Book of Flowers

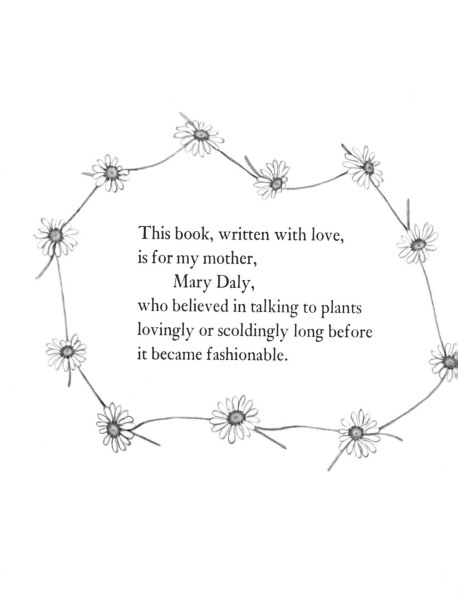

This book, written with love,
is for my mother,
      Mary Daly,
who believed in talking to plants
lovingly or scoldingly long before
it became fashionable.

A Book of
Flowers

Kathleen N. Daly

Illustrated by Susan Carlton Smith

SACRUM PRESS
Durham, North Carolina

Library of Congress Cataloging in Publication Data

Daly, Kathleen N.
  A book of flowers.

Originally published: A child's book of flowers. Garden City, N.Y.:
Doubleday, c1976.
  SUMMARY: Introduces briefly a variety of common flowers
including the dandelion, columbine, wood sorrel, rose, and
others.
  I. Flowers. [I. Flowers]
I. Smith, Susan Carlton, ill.   II. Title.
QK50.D34   1986   582.13   86-60378
ISBN 0-937543-00-4

Contents

A Note About Names 7
Flowers and
  How They Grow 8
Daisies 11
Black-eyed Susan and
  Oxeye Daisy 12
Sunflower 13
Asters 14
Goldenrod 14
Garden Flowers 15
Dandelion 16
Chicory 17
Thistle 18
Heather 19
Clover 20
Roses 21
Buttercups 22
Violets 23
Orchids 24
A Spring Bouquet 26

Mallows 28
Water Lily 29
Butter-and-eggs (Toadflax) 30
Mullein 30
Bellflower (Harebell) 31
Fireweed
  (Rose Bay Willow Herb) 32
Columbines 33
Wild Strawberry 34
Morning Glory and
  Bindweed 35
Iris 36
Poppies 37
Queen Anne's Lace 38
Honeysuckle 39
Forget-me-not 40
Wood Sorrel 41
Scientific Names of the Flowers
  in This Book 42

A Note About Names

PEOPLE love flowers so much that they give them names just as if they were human beings or pets. Since many different names may be given to a flower by people living in different parts of the world, it is useful to know the Latin, or scientific name of each flower, which is the same, no matter where it grows.

For example, the European garden daisy is also known as bairnwort or childing daisy, lawn daisy or English daisy, May gowan, March daisy, herb Margaret, boneflower, or ewe-gowan. Scientists call it *Bellis perennis*. In Latin that means "always beautiful," which is perhaps as good a name as any.

You will find the Latin names of the flowers in this book on page 42.

Flowers and How They Grow

A FLOWER is usually the prettiest part of a plant. Bees and other insects visit the flower to drink its sweet juice, called nectar.

The bees get dusted with pollen from inside the flower. They carry the pollen to other blossoms. If the pollen lands in the right place (called the stigma), seeds will start growing in the ovary below.

A fruit or a hard shell or a pod may form around the seed. Animals such as people and birds and squirrels eat the fruit and throw the seeds away. Or the wind may carry the seed away. Or the seed may stick to an animal's hair. Or the seed may pop out of its dry pod and land far away.

Inside each seed is a tiny new plant. If the seed lands in a place where it can grow, it will open up and push roots into the ground and a shoot into the air.

If there is enough water and sunlight, the tiny plant will grow to be a big one and there will be more flowers and more seeds.

People and other animals need plants to eat. And besides, they are beautiful to look at.

Plant some seeds or bulbs in a pot or in a window box. Care for them, and watch them grow. A new green shoot is a happy sight!

But don't pick wild flowers, unless you are sure there are lots and lots of them growing nearby. They are growing where Nature put them. Leave them alone, so they can send out their seeds to grow, and so that everyone who passes by may enjoy them.

Make a daisy chain for someone you love.

Daisies

THERE are lots of different kinds of daisy,
in many sizes and colors.
The name daisy means "day's eye." Many
daisies fold up their petals when the sun goes down.
These small, short daisies grow close to the
ground in tight-leaved clumps. They are called
garden daisies or English daisies.

 open   closed

Black-eyed Susan

Oxeye Daisy

SUSAN
CARLTON
SMITH

Black-eyed Susan and Oxeye Daisy

THERE are tall daisies too. Black-eyed
Susan has gay yellow petals around her one black
"eye."

The oxeye daisy has white petals around a
yellow eye.

To find out if someone loves you, pull out a
daisy's petals one by one, and say, "He loves me,
he loves me not."

The very last petal will tell you the answer!

Garden Sunflower

Wild Sunflower

SUSAN
CARLTON
SMITH

Sunflower

THE giant of all flowers is the sunflower.
It may grow taller than a tall man!
Birds love to eat its seeds, and cattle too,
enjoy sunflower-oil cake for a treat.

13

Aster (large)

Goldenrod

Aster (sma...

Goldenrod

Tᴀʟʟ, yellow goldenrods carpet miles of land in summer. The pollen dust from the thousands of tiny flowers makes some people sneeze, though many kinds of goldenrod smell sweet and do no harm.

Asters

Aꜱᴛᴇʀꜱ bloom late in the autumn, long after other flowers are dead. Sometimes they are called Michaelmas daisies. (The feast of St. Michael is on September 29.)

Marigold

Zinnia

Chrysanthemum

Garden Flowers

Many of the beautiful flowers in flower
shops and in gardens belong to the daisy family.

Dandelion

THE name dandelion means "dent-de-lion" or lion's tooth. If you look at the leaves you will see the "teeth." Like a lion, the yellow dandelion is strong and handsome. Its feathery seeds fly away in the breeze—or on your breath. They will settle down almost anywhere and grow strong roots.

What time is it?
See how many puffs it takes
to blow the seeds away!

Chicory

ANOTHER member of the daisy family, and
with leaves rather like a dandelion's, is the sky-blue
chicory. Its flowers close up on dull days, but
usually it is a cheerful sight in summer and fall.

Thistle

B<small>E</small> CAREFUL not to walk barefoot where
thistles grow, for their leaves are prickly. When the
handsome purple flowers fade you will find seeds
of softest thistledown. They float away on the
wind to find a place to take root.

Heather

THIS sturdy little plant with woody stems forms a purple carpet over hills and mountains. It is good to lie in a bed of heather, sheltered from the wind. Bees make rich honey from its flowers. Cranberries and blueberries belong to the same family as heather.

Red Clover

White Clover

SUSAN
CARLTON
SMITH

Clover

SWEET clover is a favorite with bees and also
with cattle. It grows far and wide. Its roots are
good for the soil so farmers like it too.
Clover plants have three leaflets, but if you keep
looking, maybe you will find a four-leaved clover.
Then you will have good luck!

Roses

SOME people think roses are the most beautiful
flowers in the world. Garden roses come in many,
many breathtaking colors, with smells that make you
happy just to be nearby.
Wild roses are simple flowers but just as
beautiful. Be careful of their sharp thorns!

Buttercups

THE buttercup, with its glossy cup the color of butter or of gold, grows almost everywhere, from early spring to late fall.

Some members of its family even grow under water.

To find out if your friend likes butter, hold a buttercup under her chin and see the golden glow on her skin!

Violets

LOOK carefully in moist, shady places in early
spring and you may be lucky enough to find the first
violets. Their leaves are large and heart-shaped and
the flowers are a beautiful purple with a delicious
smell. There are white and yellow violets too.
Lots of little flowers can nestle in a couple of
violet leaves to make a pretty posy. Tie it with a
ribbon.

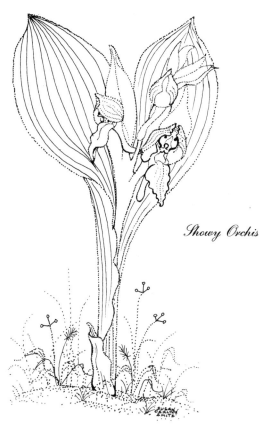

Showy Orchis

Orchids

O RCHIDS are often thought of as the kings and queens among flowers. They come in many different sizes and shapes, some of them very hard to find.

If you are lucky enough to come across a lady's-slipper or a bee orchid, don't pick it, for orchids do not grow easily. Besides, it looks better just where Nature put it!

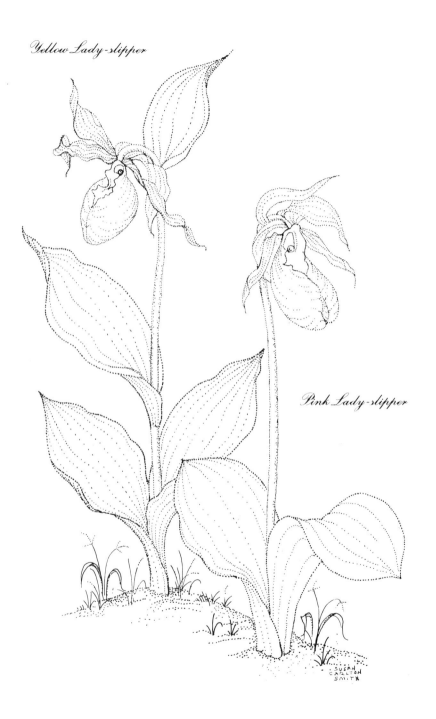

Yellow Lady-slipper

Pink Lady-slipper

SUSAN
CARLTON
SMITH

25

Snowdrop

Crocus

A Spring Bouquet

AMONG the first flowers to appear after the long winter months are the delicate white snowdrop, the crocus (white, purple, or gold), yellow daffodils, stately tulips, and sweet-smelling narcissus, hyacinth, and lily-of-the-valley.

All of these lovely flowers may easily be grown indoors in a pot or a window box. What a delicious present for someone you love!

wflake

Tulip

Narcissus

Daffodil

Wild Grape
Hyacinth

Lily of the valley

Hyacinth

Mallows

STURDY, gay mallows often grow near
the edge of the road, where their leaves get tattered
and dusty. The marsh mallow gave its name to the
marshmallows that we eat. Some mallow seeds are
good to chew and are called "fairy cheeses."

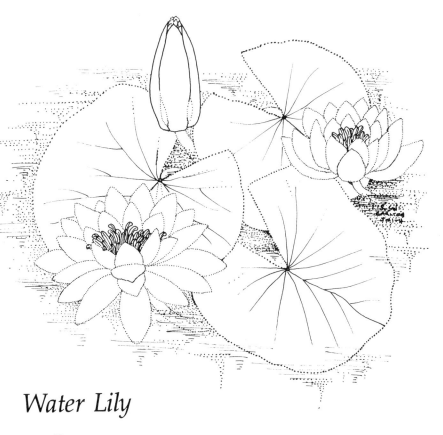

Water Lily

IF YOU were a frog or a dragonfly you'd think that a water-lily pad was the perfect place to sun yourself. The broad leaf lies flat upon the water, and the beautiful flower scents the summer air. Some bloom during the day, others open only at night.

These royal-looking flowers grow on still ponds and lakes all over the world.

Butter-and-eggs (Toadflax)

THIS handsome flower, with its lemon-colored spikes and friendly face, is given many names by children who like to pinch its "nose." Some call it snap dragon, some, bunny nose, or toadflax.

MULLEIN

Butter-and-eggs is related to the common mullein, whose yellow flowers are set on tall, straight spikes. Mulleins grow vigorously on waste places, no matter how dry or dusty the ground.

Bellflower (Harebell)

THESE delicate little flowers on their slender stalks are the bluebells-of-Scotland, where some people say you can hear the bells tinkling for fairy feasts and balls.

Fireweed (Rose Bay Willow Herb)

PURPLE rocket, firetop, blooming sally, Indian wickup—people call fireweed by many names, for it is well loved practically all over the world.

It has the kindly habit of springing up very soon after land has been burned by fire. It covers waste lands and all kinds of empty spaces. Entire hillsides may seem flaming pink when the fireweed is in flower, and smoky white when the shaggy seeds appear.

Columbines

COLUMBINES, too, have many names:
jack-in-trousers, meeting house, clucky, bells. The
pretty, graceful flowers look like little nodding
bells. Butterflies and moths, as well as bees, love to
visit columbines. Their long tongues can reach into
the long spur that holds sweet nectar.

Wild Strawberry

WILD strawberries are much smaller than the
ones we find in shops. But they are much sweeter,
too, and just the right size if you are a chipmunk
or a bird or even you.

They belong to the same family as apples and
pears and other members of the big, beautiful rose
family.

Morning Glory and Bindweed

BOTH these flowers have twining, climbing, trailing stems, which make tangled garlands on walls and pretty carpets underfoot. Their funnel-shaped blossoms, blue or white or pink, usually close before noon.

Iris

SHOWY and strangely shaped, irises grow
wild in many parts of the world. Some are white,
some gold, some purple or blue. Be careful not to
cut your hands on the iris's stiff, sharp leaves—
they are like little swords.

Poppies

BIG, floppy yellow poppies used to grow all
over California hills, and some say this is why
California was named "The Golden West."
The European poppy is brilliant red. Its seed
capsule looks like a tiny pepper pot. If you turn
it upside down you can sprinkle the black seeds
out like pepper.

Queen Anne's Lace

THE creamy blossoms of this lovely, lacy flower make a snowy carpet over fields in summer. They belong to a large family whose name means "umbrella"—if you look at the shape of the collection of blossoms you will see why.

Many of Queen Anne's relatives are good to eat as herbs and vegetables (carrots and parsley, for example). Others are very bad indeed (poison hemlock, for instance).

Never, never eat leaves or berries or flowers unless you know for sure which are good and which are not.

Honeysuckle

ONE of the sweetest of all summer smells is
that of the honeysuckle. Even its name tastes good!
Insects love it and swarm around its nectar-filled
yellow trumpets.
Honeysuckle plants have strong woody stems
that twine in a tangle around trees.
In autumn its seed berries are bright red.

Forget-me-not

THESE flowers are small, but they make up
for it by growing in great clumps or "beds,"
sometimes with their feet in a stream. The petals
are sky-blue, the centers yellow.

Each tiny face seems to say,

"Though I am small, forget me not!"

Wood Sorrel

ANOTHER tiny, but welcome plant is
wood sorrel, which grows in all kinds of waste
places. Sometimes it may completely cover a tree
stump, and it springs up in cracks between stones.
Its beautifully shaped, cloverlike leaves droop and
fold in the evening and before rain.

Scientific Names of the Flowers in This Book

English Daisy *Bellis perennis* 10-11
Black-eyed Susan *Rudbeckia hirta* 12
Oxeye Daisy *Chrysanthemum leucanthemum* 12
Garden Sunflower *Helianthus annuus* 13
Wild Sunflower *Helianthus tomentosus* 13
Aster (large) *Aster patens* 14
    (small) *Aster spectabilis* 14
Goldenrod *Solidago flexicaulis* 14
Marigold *Tagetes patula, T. erecta* 15
Zinnia *Zinnia elegans, Z. linearis* 15
Chrysanthemum *Chrysanthemum coccineum,
  C. morifolium* 15
Dandelion *Taraxacum officinale* 16
Chicory *Cichorium intybus* 17
Scottish Thistle *Cirsium vulgare* 18
Scottish Heather *Calluna vulgaris* 19
White Clover *Trifolium repens* 20
Red Clover *Trifolium pratense* 20
Wild Rose *Rosa carolina* 21
Wild Buttercup *Ranunculus bulbosus* 22
Violet (Sweet Violet) *Viola odorata* 23
Orchid (Showy orchis) *Orchis spectabilis* 24
    (Lady's-slipper) Yellow, *Cypripedium
      calceolus;* Pink, *C. acaule* 25
Crocus *Crocus sieberi, C. angustifolius* 26,27
Snowdrop *Galanthus nivalis* 26
Snowflake *Leucojum aestivum* 27
Tulip *Tulipa gesnerana* 27
Lily-of-the-Valley *Convallaria majalis* 27
Hyacinth *Hyacinthus orientalis* 27

Wild Grape Hyacinth   *Muscari botryoides*   27
Daffodil   *Narcissus pseudo-narcissus*   27
Narcissus   *Narcissus poeticus*   27
Mallow   *Hibiscus moscheutos*   28
Water Lily   *Nymphaea odorata*   29
Butter-and-eggs (Toadflax)   *Linaria vulgaris*   30
Mullein   *Verbascum thapsus*   30
Bellflower (Harebell)   *Campanula rotundifolia*   31
Fireweed   *Epilobium angustifolium*   32
Columbine   *Aquilegia canadensis*   33
Wild Strawberry   *Fragaria virginiana*   34
Morning Glory   *Ipomoea pandurata*   35
Bindweed (Low)   *Calystegia sepium*   35
Iris (wild iris)   *Iris cristata*   36
Poppy (red poppy)   *Papaver rhoeas*   37
Queen Anne's Lace   *Daucus carota*   38
Coral Honeysuckle   *Lonicera sempervirens*   39
Honeysuckle (white, yellow)   *Lonicera japonica*   39
Forget-me-not   *Myosotis scorpioides*   40
Wood Sorrel   *Oxalis acetosella*   41

NOTE: The bee shown on pp. 18, 19, 30, and 31 is a bumble bee, or *Bombus americanorum*. On p. 19, the bee is wearing the McIntosh tartan kilt and regalia. On p. 18, it is wearing the Hay tartan tam-o'-shanter. On p. 31 the bee is wearing the clan Chattan tartan tam-o'-shanter.

The ladybug, or ladybird, shown throughout the book is *Adalia bipunctata*.

About the Author

KATHLEEN N. DALY was born in London but spent her childhood on the island of Mauritius, in the Indian Ocean, and in France and Scotland. Ms. Daly has been a children's book editor in both England and America, and is the author of more than sixty books for children, many of them on the plants and animals of the world. She now makes her home in New York City.

About the Artist

SUSAN CARLTON SMITH, Assistant Curator at Duke University's Medical Center Library's Trent Collection, in Durham, North Carolina, has an extensive background as a biological and scientific illustrator. Ms. Smith has illustrated several children's books, including *Ladybug, Ladybug,* by Kathleen Daly. In addition to book illustration, Ms. Smith does scientific illustrations for the Botany Department at Duke.